Cranbury
Public
Library

23 North Main St. • Cranbury, NJ 08512
(609) 655-0555

D1518062

WE CAN READ about NATURE!™

WATER ALL AROUND

by CATHERINE NICHOLS

BENCHMARK BOOKS

MARSHALL CAVENDISH
NEW YORK

With thanks to
Susan Jefferson, first grade teacher at Miamitown
Elementary, Ohio, for sharing her innovative teaching
techniques in the Fun with Phonics section.

Benchmark Books
Marshall Cavendish Corporation
99 White Plains Road
Tarrytown, New York 10591
Website: www.marshallcavendish.com

Photo Research by Candlepants, Inc.

Cover Photo: Corbis/Stuart Westmorland

The photographs in this book are used by permission and through the courtesy of: *Corbis:*
Richard Hamilton Smith, 4, 17; Douglas Peebles, 5; Julie Habel, 6, 27; Annie Griffiths
Belt, 7 (top); Paul A. Souders, 7 (bottom); Liba Taylor, 8; Reflections Photolibrary, 9; W.
Perry Conway, 10; Natalie Fobes, 11; Gallo Images, 12, 23 (bottom); Wolfgang Kaehler,
13 (top); Adam Woolfitt, 13 (bottom); Lynda Richardson, 14; Ed Young, 15; Robert
Pickett, 16; Japack Company, 18; W. Perry Conway, 19; Philip James Corwin, 20; Bob
Krist, 21; Tim Page, 22; Diego Lezama Orezzoli, 23 (top); Galen Rowell, 24; Jim
Zuckerman, 26; Walter Hodges, 28-29.

Library of Congress Cataloging-in-Publication Data

Nichols, Catherine.
Water all around / by Catherine Nichols.
p. cm. – (We can read about nature)
Includes index (p.32).
ISBN 0-7614-1256-5
1. Water—Juvenile literature. [1. Water.] I. Title. II. Series.

GB662.3.N52 2001   551.46—dc21   2001025428

Printed in Italy

1 3 5 6 4 2

Look for us inside this book.

bubble
dew
drop
cloud
liquid
ocean
river
snow
snowflake
snowman
steam
vapor
wave

Water is all around you.
Take a look.
It's the dew on a web and

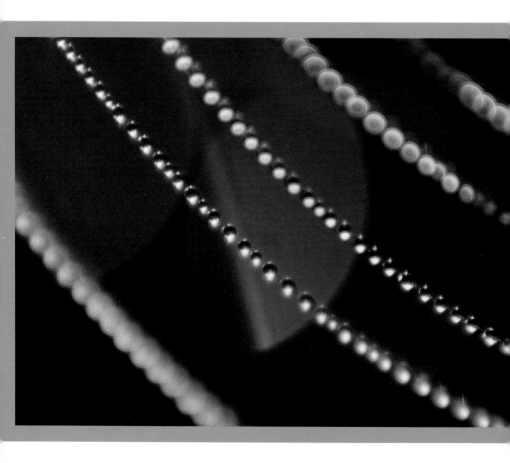

the waves on the ocean.

Water is a liquid.
You can splash it,

float on it,

and blow bubbles with it.

Water is good for drinking

and for washing dirty hands.

Sometimes water gets dirty.

The water in this river is brown.
It's no longer safe to drink.

Animals need water.

13

And so do plants.

Thanks to water, these tomatoes grew big and red.

When water freezes,
it becomes solid.

Where is the water here . . .

and here?

Tweeeee!
The water in this kettle is boiling.
The heat changes the water
into vapor.
When hot vapor meets cold air,
steam is formed.

What's happening here?
The same thing.
Deep inside the earth hot rocks
heat water.
Vapor rushes out.

Tiny drops of water, too small to see,
make up these clouds.
The drops join together and make
bigger drops.

Now the drops are falling.
It's raining.
Time to open an umbrella!

Sometimes too much rain falls.

Other times
not enough.
Then the ground
becomes dry
and cracked.

Plants can't grow.

Brrrr!
It's cold outside.
Snow is falling.

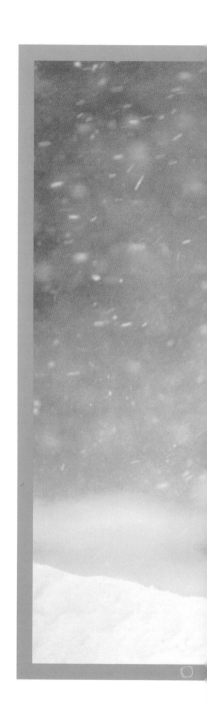

Snow is made of snowflakes.

How many snowflakes did it take
to build this snowman?

Wherever you are and whatever you do, water is all around you!